THROUGH THE VALLEY

HOW PSALM 23 GIVES US HOPE IN SUFFERING

ROB WOOTTON

White Blackbird
BOOKS

PRAISE FOR THROUGH THE VALLEY

Through the Valley is filled with hospitable warmth, courageous honesty, deep conviction, and empathetic understanding. Like a shepherd, Rob guides us through Psalm 23 by leading us through his experience and feasting on this Scripture. He shows how the Good Shepherd is the only comfort and hope. *Through the Valley* blessed me and will now be a resource I draw from for offering others hope.

Sarah Viggiano Wright
Counselor, Global Counseling Network
Author, *A Living Hope: A Study of 1 Peter*

In *Through the Valley*, Rob Wootton teaches on Psalm 23 in a fresh and insightful way, and he addresses the ever-relevant topic of suffering with deep pastoral wisdom and care as he points the reader to Jesus, the True Great Shepherd.

Owen Lee
Pastor, Christ Central Presbyterian Church

Rob Wootton's *Through the Valley* is not just a biblical or theological study on Psalm 23, although Rob certainly does good biblical work on the passage. And as powerful as it is that Rob shares much of his own personal story and suffering, this work is not only that. Rob's work invites us to know and experience the Shepherd ourselves, bringing our own personal stories and suffering to him. I am personally blessed, challenged, and comforted by entering in to the valley where Rob invites us to meet the Lord. I am happy to pass this work along to people in my community and congregation who are suffering.

Thurman Williams

Pastor, New City Fellowship

Human suffering is inevitable because Genesis 3 is in the Bible. However, Psalm 23 is in the Bible too. Autobiographically and narratively, Rob, methodically and pastorally, takes us as weak little lambs and gives us a tour of this beautiful piece of poetry for a beautiful end: so that we will have hope in our spiritual tanks when the inevitable happens—an appointment with suffering. Please give this book your unhurried meditative time and attention. Your soul and those you love will thank you.

Luke Bobo

Visiting Professor of Contemporary Culture
Covenant Theological Seminary

What's it like to walk through life getting wrung up and wrung out? How in the world does one make it through? Rob Wootton writes as one who has been through the wringer—more than once! *Through the Valley* captures his exploration with Psalm 23 and the Good Shepherd, whose goodness and mercy pursue us even when we trudge through the valley of the shadow of death. These thoughtful meditations will help with the stings and hurts so that Psalm 23 soothes your soul.

Michael W. Philliber
Pastor, Heritage Presbyterian Church
Author, *To You I Lift Up My Soul*

If you find your life filled with valleys and shadows, Psalm 23 is a mainstay. In this short prayer, there are riches that connect us to God's presence, care, and future. These make life not only bearable, but rich. Rob has done a terrific job helping us to mine those riches.

Scott Sauls
Pastor, Christ Presbyterian Church
Author, *Jesus Outside the Lines* and *A Gentle Answer*

Two truths become clear reading *Through the Valley*: Rob has suffered, and he knows the Good Shepherd. Vulnerability and confidence combine in his writing and make him an excellent teacher, one a reader can trust. Walking the difficult line of sharing honestly without belaboring grief for effect or revealing too much, Rob tells his stories in order to draw the reader toward relationship with his words and, most importantly, with Jesus. Short, sweet, and deep, this book will land on many a bedside table, dog-eared, pencil-marked, and frequently visited.

Jessica Ribera
Author, *The Almost Dancer*

In trials and chaos, people do not have an adequate understanding of suffering as a part of the Christian life.

But Psalm 23 shows us how the Good Shepherd not only uses the valley for his glory in our lives, but how he gives his goodness to us in ways that we otherwise could not see or receive. Rob Wootton walks us through his own times of trials and suffering as he opens Psalm 23 to get closer to Jesus our Great, Good Shepherd so that our own sufferings will become crucibles of God's hope and joy in time.

Eric Lazarian
Deacon, Citylife Presbyterian Church

If you have been to the Valley of the Shadow, you will connect to Wootton's stories and reflections. He knows well the endless, white-knuckled times of terror and tears. In moments where pious platitudes failed him and where his own resources were not nearly enough, he grabbed hold of the 23rd Psalm. He began to find fresh hope in the tough, tender care of his Shepherd. When the pain was too great to muscle through, he discovered a mission larger than his comfort. God was offering him a fresh peace that was not escape, a contentment that was not complacency. In this great psalm, Wootton gradually discovered a readiness to face deep darkness and a love directed not toward material success but to the arms of the Good Shepherd himself. He found deeper joy in the God who was willing to enter into our pain in order to lead us to a better place. Wootton is a thoughtful, sensitive, and faithful guide to the most beloved poem God has given us. Wootton is a master storyteller, a careful exegete, and a kind truth teller. Whether the reader is a seasoned Christ-follower or a skeptic still test-driving the faith, this book is a roadmap through the valley to the Shepherd's embrace.

Ray Cannata
Pastor, Redeemer Church
Author, *Rooted*

Through Rob Wootton's work on the 23rd Psalm, we do not just get another intellectual overview but an existential entrance into this beautiful piece of poetry. He offers real hope over false peace by revealing that going through suffering, rather than avoiding it, is deep work of God's goodness. As he pulls back the veil of his own life, letting us in on the suffering in his own story, he reveals redemption that is better than perfection.

Jim Pocta
Pocta Counseling

Through the Valley by Rob Wootton may be the sweetest exposition of Psalm 23 I have ever read. It is honest and delightfully resistant to a formulaic Christianity. Instead it speaks to a God who "draws us into his inner circle, bringing us into the intimacy the Father, Son, and Spirit share." I was riveted by his recollection of when he nearly drowned in the ocean and warmed by the permission he gives to freely admit our fears because the Lord is our Shepherd. This will be a resource that I draw upon, both in the pulpit, and in my own life as a Christ-follower.

Mike Khandjian
Pastor, Chapelgate Presbyterian Church
Author, *A Sometimes Stumbling Life*

The beauty of Scripture, even if one has walked on a well-worn path of a particular passage or chapter, is that there are always new depths to plumb and vistas to behold. It's even better to take that journey when you have a wise, compassionate, and experienced guide walking with you. In *Through the Valley*, Rob Wootton is that guide for us as he walks with us through Psalm 23 and how the Good Shepherd has met him there again and again, especially in his most painful and difficult seasons of his life. In so doing, he helps us to see how our Lord and Shepherd will meet us where we are and guide us through our lives. For that, I am grateful for Rob opening up his life and pointing us to Jesus.

Adam Tisdale
Pastor, North Hills Church
Cancer Survivor

The experience of suffering is a spiritual fork in the road for many of us. Life in the valley of suffering tries and tests us. If you're open to pressing into the Good Shepherd more deeply in the midst of trials, heartbreak, and disappointment, this book is a lifeline. Rob is honest about the difficulties he's faced, yet what gets celebrated in these pages is not the despair and the pain but the faithfulness of God, who walks with us through the challenges. Give it a read and let Rob help you meet the same God that has met him through the richness of Psalm 23.

Alex Kirk
Pastor, Chatham Community Church
General Editor, *The Small Group Leader's Handbook*

While most of us have read Psalm 23, many of us don't really understand it. We think it is a psalm about dying. But *Through the Valley* shows us it is really about living. Rob's insights and reflections help us understand the depth of riches in Psalm 23. It is a valuable resource to help us learn how to pray, how to suffer, and how to live in the presence of God. I encourage you to read this book again and again and again—until you have internalized what it means to trust the Lord as your Good Shepherd.

Brad Houff
Director, Compass Center for Christian Formation & Leadership

Rob has written a biblically sound, pastoral, and practical book for those who are suffering and longing for healing. He understands the depths of hardships while also experiencing the caring pursuit of our Good Shepherd. This book will help you feel as if you were listening to the kind, intimate, and hopeful comfort of our Savior, Jesus Christ. As a licensed professional counselor, I am thrilled to have this book as a resource for my clients, especially as they try to make sense of their own suffering.

Mark Pfuetze
Professor, Co-Director, Master of Arts in Counseling Program, Covenant Theological Seminary

Many people have suffered in this life, and this always leads to questions regarding God's claim to be both all-powerful and good. While there are those who have had a shipwrecked faith, others have emerged from this suffering with their beliefs deepened and strengthened. The well-known 23rd Psalm provides us with a window into the incredible goodness of God and his commitment to not only care for us in the midst of our suffering but to actually be with us. As a pastor, student of Scripture, and fellow sufferer, Rob does an excellent job of drawing us into a familiar psalm with both pastoral and experiential insight. Suffering is a reality we all experience, and I hope this work will be an aid to you in answering how we suffer well and with hope because of our great God.

Dennis Hermerding

Pastor, King's Cross Church

Contributing Author, *Heal Us Emmanuel*

CONTENTS

For Abi, Nate, Naomi, and Miriam—
You have shown me the joy of loving and serving others.

For Robin—
You are more than I could have hoped and dreamed.

FOREWORD

REV. JAY SIMMONS

Let's be honest, shall we? We do not want to walk through the *Valley of the Shadow of Death*. If you are like me, you spend energy, time, money, vocational pursuits, and relational navigations steering clear of that valley. If we are suffering in it, we try to climb out, pushing ourselves and our rocks of accumulation, comfort, and ease up the steep cliffs with us. We become like Sisyphus of Greek mythology fame, each day sliding back down into its depths. In our own strength, with our wits, and through our lies, we push, scamper, and compartmentalize. We numb ourselves into exhaustion, cynicism, and despair. Ultimately, we find we cannot make it out. We discover that the valley is our reality, and that the valley is an honest part of our lives. Our real lives.

Psalm 23 has long been a place to catch our breath after those fruitless efforts. It is a place of surrender and yielding. We see in its words a king, King David, who had more of the human capacities for self-saving than we employ in our attempts to escape the valley. David remained still and faced the truth about himself, his heart, and his journey through real life. From there, he found the courage and wisdom to release the lie of his own ability to save himself. He discovered the strength to follow his Good Shepherd through the valley, knowing he is loved and protected.

As I allowed my own story through the valley to sink into the pages of this wonderful little book, I found the same strange joy and peace that David must have felt in writing Psalm 23. I also found new courage to follow the Lord once again.

Rob Wootton is a trusted guide through this process. I have known Rob for almost twenty years and have had the privilege and pain of watching him and sometimes walking with him through his own valley of the shadow of death. During one of his darkest moments, I got a call from him as he was riding his bike through the streets of Seattle. Huffing and puffing amidst tears, longings, and fears, he needed a friend to hear his heart and a fellow sheep who could remind him that he was not alone in this valley. Rob needed to know that he had a Good Shepherd leading him through the darkest moments of life.

Rob is reliably, unashamedly authentic about his own struggles and anxieties. This is a quality I have long admired in him. It is refreshing in a day where honesty about our pain is hard to come by. I have learned to expect this from Rob, and it is an aspect of his character that has taught me as I struggle with my own dark valleys. Rob's courage to lay open his own life led me through these pages, inviting me into the same comfort and assurance he needed from me on the day of that phone call. It is the comfort and assurance that comes through surrendering and following our Lord.

Rob has returned the favor to a fellow sheep, reminding me that I am not alone in my valley. In these pages and with his help, I found the courage and wisdom to be honest with myself. I found the strength to face the truth about this dark world, its sin, and the gloom and fear of this real life I inhabit. I also discovered the joy and peace needed to follow once again.

If you are daring enough to stop the impossible climb of pushing yourself and your rocks out of the valley, then let Rob, King David, and most importantly, the Lord lead you through your suffering. If you surrender to the Good Shepherd's gentle care, you will find in these pages the still waters you are longing for, just like I did.

As a pastor, this book will be on the top of my "go-to" stack, as it not only reminds me of my own need but also provides a great resource for all of those I minister to day after day who are exhausted trying to climb their way out of the valley in their own strength. I know it will be a needed reminder and a vital respite for their struggling souls, and I will recommend it again and again.

Jay Simmons
Pastor, All Souls Church

INTRODUCTION

For as long as I can remember, my family faithfully attended the Methodist church where we lived in Roanoke, Virginia. The church was just one block down a gentle hill on a tree-lined street not too far from downtown. In our small city tucked away in the Appalachian Mountains, we enjoyed these family walks down the street on Sundays, particularly on fall days with pleasant temperatures with the trees in their autumn glory. I still have a picture of us all after church one Sunday looking like proper churchgoing folk with smiles on our faces. My father and I wore ties, and my mother and sister in pretty dresses.

Growing up in a Methodist church meant you went to a confirmation class where preteens are instructed on what it means to be a part of their church. I do not remember anything about the class, but I do recall standing in front of the church when all the classes were complete. We were asked to recite Psalm 23. We had learned it in the old King James Version with words like "thy," "thou," "maketh," "leadeth," and "restoreth." I stood in front of the congregation and proudly recited the psalm without any faults. At the end, I received a burgundy fake-leather Bible with my name embossed on the lower right of the front cover. There was polite church clapping, and the next eleven- or twelve-year-old did the same.

Perhaps you did not grow up in church or have never been in church. Still, you have heard the part of Psalm 23 that goes, *"The Lord is my shepherd,"* or *"Even though I walk through the valley of the shadow of death,"* but you only vaguely recall that it belongs to the Bible, much less a psalm. If you are searching for something greater and bigger than yourself, and you are not sure whether the Bible is the place to find it, then you are in the right place. We all long for a "Never-Stopping, Never Giving Up, Unbreaking, Always and Forever Love,"[1] even if we cannot express it with those words. Take a risk and consider how this little book (and more importantly Psalm 23 itself) might be the doorway to the answers you are looking for.

Perhaps you had a similar experience to mine growing up and have long known the prominent place Psalm 23 holds in the Christian community. If you can recite it without making a mistake, and the words roll off your tongue with ease, it might be easy to forget its beauty and significance. Maybe you have read it a hundred times, heard many sermons from Psalm 23, and led Bible studies and prayer times in Psalm 23. If any of these, or something like them, are true of you, then this book is for you. May you recapture the heart of the Good Shepherd and remember again the promises of "God's Never-Stopping, Never Giving Up, Unbreaking, Always and Forever Love."

This psalm is one of the most, if not *the* most, influential poems of history. It figures proximately in Islam as well as Judaism and Christianity.[2] More four billion people in these religious communities have some familiarity with this piece of poetry.

I wrote this book to share with you how Psalm 23 has impacted my life so deeply and powerfully. It is not too much to say this psalm saved my life. A friend and mentor told me recently that we do not need more illustrations, but we need more stories. My stories illustrate what I hope to communicate about Psalm 23, but they are not illustrations. I am inviting you into my story with the hope that Psalm 23 becomes a part of yours.

Some of you may want to skip from story to story. That is okay, but please do not forget Psalm 23, and please consider King David's story which led him to write this song. Some of you may want to skip the stories and get right to the teaching. Let me invite you to slow down, to enter into David's story, your story, and mine. I do share my twenty-five years of ministry experience and with it the training and study, which is critical to my work. But without stories, it is easy to miss the heart of the teaching.

This book is from my life, and my prayer is that you will draw closer to the Good Shepherd. I hope you write all over this book—your thoughts, the connections made with your own story, and how it brings you closer to God. At the end of each chapter, I have included some questions for further study and reflection to help in this process. If it is impactful for you, will you consider buying a copy for someone else who might need it? I'm not asking so I can sell more books, but so your friends can find hope here as well.

If you are new to Psalm 23 or are considering it again in a new stage of life, I am praying as I write this that you would find in this psalm the same hope I do.

———

As we make our way through together, I would like you to consider these three questions:

- How can we begin to suffer well?
- How can a good God allow suffering?
- How can we suffer with hope?

HOW CAN WE SUFFER WELL?

The ordination process in my denomination (The Presbyterian Church in America) is extensive and often-times grueling. It is comparable to the bar exam for lawyers or the boards that doctors take. For those working toward becoming a Presbyterian minister, the process consists of five or six written exams. These cover theology, Bible, sacraments, church governance, church history, and their application to pastoral work. Each exam can take up to three or four hours. If you pass those written tests, you sit before a committee of six to ten people who then grill you with new questions. They are free to ask you follow-up questions from your written work, particularly about the ones you missed. If you pass the committee exam, you go before the floor of the regional governing body with fifty to one hundred pastors and elders who then ask you more questions related to the written tests, the committee exams, and anything else they wish.

When I was finishing my last semester in seminary, I

was asked to start a new church in Seattle. I was taking a full course load, working to pass all my ordination exams, and raising money for the new church.

Not all my motives were pure. Pride had compelled me to pursue this heavy load because it would garner me the respect I so desperately craved.

A few weeks later, I learned I had failed the written portion of the English Bible exam.

It was humbling. I had just spent three years studying the Bible at a graduate-degree level. I may have mixed up the order of Old Testament minor prophets. Perhaps I could not remember where and when certain events took place. It is likely I could not list the twelve disciples with their alternate names. But the most jarring mistake I made was that I could not write out Psalm 23.

I knew it. As I wrote above, I had it previously memorized since childhood. But when I came to this exam, I could not get it right.

It was not the end of my pursuit of ordination. A few months later I passed all the written, committee, and floor exams. And as I prepared for these exams again I made sure I knew Psalm 23. I wrote it out at least one hundred times. I recited it aloud again and again. Whether or not it was engraved on my soul, I made sure it was on my mind.

Now, I am thankful I failed the Bible exam and had to relearn Psalm 23. The suffering that was soon to come, suffering that was more intense than anything I had experienced, required the knowledge and the heart of Psalm 23.

Suffering is a part of life. We know this is true, but we hate anything that brings discomfort. To avoid these pains, we close our hearts to our own suffering and the suffering of others. When we do, we have bought into our culture of success, prosperity, comfort, and ease, even if we rarely experience these things. They have become our highest good. When anything comes along that challenges us, like something that does not feel good, we automatically throw up walls to protect ourselves.

We know we will always face some type of suffering, challenge, or difficulty in this broken world, yet we run from these difficulties as quickly as we can. For many of us, it is not hard to recall some distant pain we would prefer to avoid.

Psalm 23 does not avoid those pains. Derek Kidner writes this about Psalm 23:

> Its peace is not escape; its contentment is not complacency: there is readiness to face deep darkness and imminent attack, and the climax reveals a love which comes towards not material goal but to the Lord Himself.[1]

We will start by looking at some of the trials of King David's life. My hope and prayer is that we will find the courage to embrace the pain of suffering of our own lives, trusting we are being led and comforted by God's goodness and mercy.

Psalm 23 was written during the time of David's suffering through his son Absalom's rebellion. That story has its beginning in David's affair with Bathsheba and the murder of her husband Uriah. We find this account in full in 2 Samuel 10–11.

David was confronted by the prophet Nathan, and David understood the depth of his sin (see Psalm 51). Part of Nathan's prophetic confrontation was the edict that David's child with Bathsheba would die, but the consequences of David sin had far-reaching implications. Nathan spoke God's words to David saying:

> *"Now therefore the sword shall never depart from your house, because you have despised me and have taken the wife of Uriah the Hittite to be your wife." Thus says the LORD, "Behold, I will raise up evil against you out of your own house."* (2 Sam. 12:10–11)

Absalom was the third son born to David about ten years prior to his affair with Bathsheba and the murder of Uriah. A few years later, the story of Absalom's rebellion begins. It is a brutal and tragic tale which we find in full in 2 Samuel 13–18.

Amnon, David's firstborn son, became tormented by his desire for Absalom's sister, Tamar. She is described as a beautiful woman, and Amnon could not resist the temptation. He pursued her with evil intent. Amnon raped his sister Tamar, and then he became disgusted with her. He threw her out, and she lived the rest of her days a desolate woman in her brother Absalom's house.

Absalom was enraged. He plotted, schemed, and then murdered his brother Amnon. When David learned of this, he tore his clothes in grief and mourning, and

Nathan's prophecy began to be fulfilled. It did not end there. The conflict between David and Absalom escalated. Eventually David fled for his life, left Jerusalem, and was chased by 12,000 men. This was the start of a civil war within Israel. Thousands fought on each side. Throughout this conflict, David longed to be reconciled with his son and ordered his commanders that Absalom was not to be harmed. The war ended with Absalom's death:

> *The king said to the Cushite, "Is it well with the young man Absalom?" And the Cushite answered, "May the enemies of my lord the king and all who rise up against you for evil be like that young man." And the king was deeply moved and went up to the chamber over the gate and wept. And as he went, he said, "O my son Absalom, my son, my son Absalom! Would I had died instead of you, O Absalom, my son, my son!"* (2 Sam. 18:32–33)

David loved deeply, and yet he brought tragedy upon tragedy to his family. Nathan's words never left David. As he mourned for Absalom, he experienced the deep pain of sin and death at work in his and his family's life. It was more than he could bear, and it is in this setting that Psalm 23 was born. During the worst pain of his life, he reminds himself of God's promises. David wrote psalms of lament, (13, 40, and others) which were songs and prayers of grief, mourning, and crying out to the LORD, "How long?"

However, Psalm 23 is not a cry of lament. It would not have been surprising if David had asked to die, expressing something like the hopelessness of Psalm 88:

> *Your wrath has swept over me;*
> *your dreadful assaults destroy me.*
> *They surround me like a flood all day long;*
> *they close in on me together.*
> *You have caused my beloved and my friend to shun me;*
> *my companions have become darkness.* (Ps. 88:16–18)

Lament would have been appropriate during his grief and pain. It would have been natural to cry out to God in sorrow and mourning, pleading to God to put an end to his sin and the heartache it had caused for him and his family.

Thus, what David does in Psalm 23 is striking because of how he moves into his great suffering and because of how he hopes and trust as he writes *"through the valley of the shadow of death."* His hope starts with the tender care of a shepherd.

The LORD is my shepherd; I shall not want.

Ministry began for me right after college, with Inter-Varsity Christian Fellowship. Ryan was one of my students and a friend. He took a semester to study in England, and he invited me over for Spring Break to explore the Scottish Highlands. I flew into Heathrow and rented a sporty Peugeot hatchback. After a few twists, turns, and roundabouts on London city streets, I was on the M40 to Birmingham to pick up Ryan.

I rented a car instead of taking a train because we wanted to get lost in the Scottish Highlands. And that we did. We did not have smart phones with Google Maps, so with paper maps in hand, we proceeded with reckless abandon. My driving was definitely reckless, though Ryan was sure and steady behind the wheel. As we sped through the Highlands, we drove on single-track roads that had turnouts for passing every half mile or so. At one point, I had to reverse for a quarter of a mile to allow another car to get by.

We did not often encounter other cars, and one day I flew around a corner over a little hill, and there were a hundred sheep on and around the road. I had plenty of time to stop, so there was not a bloody mutton accident. As I slowly approached this flock, the sheep gave us and our car no notice. They deafly, blindly, and stupidly stood there as I honked the horn and inched closer and closer. I even carefully nudged one with the bumper, and it jumped out of the way, but there were still a hundred more happy to ignore us.

We got out of the car and waved our arms. We yelled and gently nudged them with our feet, not kicking but gently pushing, eventually clearing a twenty-five-foot path big enough to drive through. As we got back in the car, we were amused and discouraged to find the flock had merged back together. The only way to get through this oblivious mass of mutton was to have Ryan wave, yell, and nudge the dumb animals as I followed closely behind in the car.

Deaf, blind, dumb, and stupid. This is often how sheep are described in sermons. The pastor eventually makes the point that we too—like sheep—are deaf, blind, dumb, and stupid. There may be some parallels to be made there, but that is not what David had in mind when he wrote Psalm 23. It is not what God had in mind with the imagery of sheep and shepherd used throughout the Bible.

As we read on, we can find great comfort as sheep in God's pasture.

Often when I lay down at night and the anxiety, fears, and troubles of the day come rushing in, I turn to Psalm 23. I remember again and again that the Lord is my Shepherd.

Sometimes though, I will rush through all six verses as though they were some type of incantation to fix my anxiety. I then try to slow down and consider each word. I emphasize each of the five words from the first phrase and consider what the different emphasis communicates about trusting The LORD is my shepherd:

THE *Lord is my shepherd*—THE one and only God of the universe. THE one who created all things. THE one who sustains all things. THE one who orders all things. HE is the one who has chosen me to be a part of his flock.

The **LORD** *is my shepherd*. In Hebrew what is translated "the LORD" is only one word, YHWY.[2] Instead of YHWY, we find "the LORD" for a few reasons. In Jewish tradition, it is forbidden to speak God's name. Instead they say *Adonai*, which is translated literally as "the Lord." Because of this tradition, when the Hebrew was translated into English we find "the LORD" (the all caps LORD is to let us know it is YHWY in Hebrew). This tradition extended into the Christian practice, and because so many have learned *"The LORD is my shepherd,"* translation teams are usually reticent to make such a significant change.

The second reason it has not been changed is because we do not know for sure how to pronounce YHWY / יְהֹוָה. The dots and dashes below the letters were not added to the Hebrew text until the Masoretes began adding vowels in the sixth through tenth centuries AD.

Considering God's name and how we say it is important because of what happened when God told his name to the prophet Moses through the burning bush. Moses had left Egypt years before and had been living the life of a shepherd. He never thought he would return to Egypt or be sent by God to rescue the Hebrew people from their slavery. That is what God had called him to do, and even though speaking with THE God of all things he was unsure of this task. We read:

> *Then Moses said to God, "If I come to the people of Israel and say to them, 'The God of your fathers has sent me to you,' and they ask me, 'What is his name?' what shall I say to them?" God said to Moses, "I AM WHO I AM." And he said, "Say this to the people of Israel: 'I AM sent me to you.'"* (Exod. 3:13–14)

The last I AM of verse 14 in the Hebrew is יְהֹוָה אֱלֹהָי, two words when changed from Hebrew letters to English are *Yahwey Elohe*, The LORD God. The previous two I AMs are a little different in the Hebrew but related to both YHWY and I AM.

I AM and YHWY are how God identifies himself. God is saying to Moses, and all of his people for all time, that he is a God who can be known. Through Psalm 23, David reminds himself and us that we can know him personally because he shares his name with us. This is not some far-off god demanding obedience, sacrifice, and worship. He is the God we can come to, who invites us to speak with him, to call out to him by name, and invites us from this relationship to follow him. As we recognize *The LORD is my shepherd*, it is not just saying he is the one and only God of the universe, the one who created all things, the one who sustains all things, and the one who orders all thing. He is those things yes, and the one who has done all this now draws us into his inner circle, bringing us into the intimacy the Father, Son, and Spirit share. He is the God who calls us to know his love as a tender shepherd.

The LORD **IS** *my shepherd.* The "is" is an extension of God sharing his name with us. It is God saying I AM. He continues to tell us about himself. It is also an addition in English that we do not find in the Hebrew. The King James Version puts the "is" in italics for this reason. A word-for-word translation is "YHWY my shepherd." For us in English, it drives home that the Lord "is" in fact the one who has called us and who has made us his flock. The one who "is" caring for us as a tender shepherd. It is both what he does and his identity.

The LORD is **MY** *shepherd.* He is not just *the* shepherd or *our* shepherd—he is *my* shepherd. I am his, and he is mine. Again, it is an extension of how God calls us. This is not a set of beliefs we have to assent to in order to be a part of his flock. It is not rituals that have to be performed to be counted as one of his people. He does not demand obedience so we can join his congregation or remain in that congregation. With every word, David reminds himself through this tragedy that he is God's, and God is his.

The LORD is my **SHEPHERD.** This rightly gets further treatment below because it is one of the central metaphors of the psalm. Commentator Derek Kidner writes:

> In the word shepherd, David uses the most comprehensive and intimate metaphor yet encountered in the Psalms, preferring usually the more distant "king" or "deliverer," or the impersonal "rock," "shield," etc.; whereas the shepherd lives with his flock and is everything to it: guide, physician, and protector.[3]

In my hopes to be reminded of these truths as I try to rest in the LORD and get to sleep, I go further with this exercise of emphasizing each word in turn. I do not often make it all the way through all six verses before I receive the gift of sleep from my Shepherd. Yet there are some nights where the anxieties and fears press in harder, and it is still because of my Shepherd that I am able to trust him during these anxieties and fears even without sleep. I write more on anxiety and fear later.

The LORD is my shepherd; I shall not want.
He makes me lie down in green pastures.
He leads me beside still waters.

We want to lie down in a place of peace where we can trust that nothing will upset our rest. Commentators Keil and Delitzsch write, "(in green pastures) according to its primary meaning, is a resting- or dwelling-place, specifically an oasis, i.e., a verdant spot in the desert."[4]

As we wander through this desert of our souls, the LORD makes us lie down and rest. We all long for soul restoration, even if we do not think it exists or that it is possible. We know in deep personal ways there has been significant and perhaps irreversible damage done to the very center of who we are. We want rest, and we need it because we know there is suffering and brokenness in this world, country, lives, families, and in our hearts. We want to find that type of rest which comes with the contentment that all our needs have been met.

W. Philip Keller worked as a shepherd for eight years and owned hundreds of sheep before pursuing a career in agricultural research and land management. In his book *A Shepherd Looks at Psalm 23*, he writes:

The strange thing about sheep is that because of their very makeup it is almost impossible for them to be made to lie down unless four requirements are met. Owing to their timidity, they refuse to lie down unless they are free of all fear. Because of their social behavior within a flock, sheep will not lie down unless they are free from friction with others of their kind. If tormented by flies or parasites, sheep will not lie down. Only when free of these pests can they relax. Lastly sheep will not lie down as long as they feel in need of finding food. They must be free from hunger.[5]

Free from fear, strife, irritation, and physical needs. It is all well and good for a hardworking shepherd to provide this for the sheep, but for us this seems like an impossibility. How can God make us rest during our personal and collective troubles?

First, we must engage with what is happening in our lives. Use this list and write out your personal fears, strife, irritations, and physical needs that are not being met:

Fear—What makes you anxious, insecure, or overwhelmed?

Strife—Where is there conflict in your life? With whom have you argued lately?

Irritation—What are some annoyances you wish you could avoid?

Physical Needs—More than just food, but health matters, living situation, safety concerns, and intimacy needs, and others fit here.

Take a moment to consider what makes you long for soul restoration. What in your life is keeping you from contentment? What keeps you from saying, "I want for nothing?"

Usually we deal with suffering by shutting ourselves off from it. We do not allow it. We escape or ignore it. We pursue anything to numb ourselves. We do this with reading, television, movies, social media, the news, food, exercise, sleep, and more. We all need a break at times from what is heavy and draining, and some of these benign pursuits provide us the break we so desperately need.

For example, I love to read fiction and find it to be a healthy way to step back from the constant demands on my life. But when that becomes a way to escape and not deal with all of life's pressures (which is too often the case), it then stops providing a break from the weighty aspects of life. Using reading to avoid something that requires my engagement and presence actually creates more anxiety. It is akin to turning up the music so you can't hear the awful sound your car makes when you drive.

Could I be addicted to reading? Anything taken too far will cease to provide what we were looking for in the first place. These pursuits then become malignant. We also pursue malignancies such as alcohol, drugs, pornography, cutting, and more because we do not want to deal with the deeper pains in our lives and our past. When we pursue both benign and malignant escapes to avoid suffering, those escapes are detriments to our souls. We are becoming less human when we pursue them to mitigate our pain. Eventually, we will become less aware of ourselves, what is happening in our lives, what is happening in the lives of those we love, and what God is doing in our lives.

Another way we cope with our internal pain is through transferring it to issues outside of ourselves. Social media and the news cycle make us experience the concerns of the country and the world more intensely than ever. Our anxiety about what is happening in the world will impact the way we handle what is happening in our own lives. It is easier to face the troubles of others than the ones in our own hearts.

If there are family issues, we might transfer our pain by saying, "I am just worried about _____." If there are cultural, national, or global issues, we might say, "There is so much going on in the world/country right now, and it is really upsetting."

These types of responses and the act of transferring our pain to someone or something else keep us from looking deeply at our need for a shepherd who promises to give us rest and to take care of all our needs. If we are transferring our pain to someone or something else we will not experience the rest God promises or our soul's restoration.

Christians face the temptation to put what I will call a Jesus band-aid on our soul pain. Instead of acknowledging the pain we quickly turn to a verse like Romans 8:28: *"And we know that for those who love God all things work together for good, for those who are called according to his purpose."*

I believe what this verse says is true, but when we

use it to try to mitigate our pain, it becomes a platitude. Merriam-Webster defines "platitude" as a "banal, trite, or stale remark."[6] Turning Romans 8:28 and others like it into these trite remarks may be nice for a cross-stitch hanging on your grandmother's wall, but it robs God's Word from the hope it proclaims. It becomes a stale remark, something you have heard before but which no longer has your attention. I will not offer this false peace that keeps us from experiencing real hope, and my prayer is that we will not accept this pretense from anywhere or anyone. God works good through our pain as we feel its weight. It is only when we embrace the depth of the darkness in the valley and in our souls that we find the real hope of light.

Sometimes we do not have the words to express the depth of the darkness in our souls. We need help understanding and naming our pain. Below are words to help us express our feelings about this present darkness. Circle the ones that best capture right now, in this moment, why you need soul restoration:

sorrow

misery

sadness

anguish

pain

distress

agony

torment

affliction

suffering

heartache

heartbreak

broken heartedness

heaviness of heart

woe

desolation

despondency

dejection

despair

angst

mourning

bereavement

lamentation

remorse

regret

longing

blue

We must think through and feel our pain. We cannot ignore it. I want us each to say, "I cannot handle it! It is too much!" Say this to God. Say it to a friend, to your spouse, your counselor, or a pastor. You need to say it out loud to God and to someone else. The truth is we cannot handle it, and it is too much, but God promises he will walk through this with each of us.

To suffer well, we have to do this hard work, and it is truly difficult to engage deep pain, especially if we have ignored it for so long. Remember the promise here. The LORD will make each of us lie down in a place of peace and rest. He will not leave us in our pain, and he will restore. One commentator puts it this way:

["My soul he restores"] signifies to bring back the soul that is as it were flown away, so that it comes to itself again, therefore to impart new life, *receare*. This he does to the soul, by causing it amidst the dryness and heat of temptation and trouble to taste the very essence of life which refreshes and strengthens it.[7]

Questions for Further Reflection and Study

- How is the "my" in *The Lord is my shepherd* more significant than if we were to substitute "our"?

- What are your usual wants? Finish this sentence: What I really want is _____.

- Has God met all your needs?

- Does the LORD need to make you lie down, make you rest, make you unplug? How are you fighting him?

- Where are the green pastures in your life? Where do you feel most at rest?

- What has damaged your soul? How can God restore your soul?

- What still needs to happen in your life for soul restoration?

HOW CAN A GOOD GOD ALLOW SUFFERING?

In January 2010, I went away for a sermon prep and prayer retreat. I spent three days in a cabin on a lake near where I was starting a new church in Seattle. My heart and soul were heavy and troubled by challenges in marriage, parenting, conflict with a colleague, and starting a new church. I felt the weight of these as I headed out of town.

Despite these troubles, I looked forward to the time alone. I planned on working through what I would preach next in this initial phase of the church. I took all the tools I needed to research and prepare for a sermon series in the book of Acts. Along with a stack of commentaries, I had Paul Miller's recently released *A Praying Life*. I enjoyed these days of prayer and study by the lake in a gray, weather-worn Adirondack chair. I walked and prayed in the cool, misty Pacific northwest. In the evenings, I sat by the fire pit and smoked my pipe, contemplating what God was up to in my life and work.

However, I could not get any traction in my sermon prep. Every time I opened my laptop or a commentary, nothing would come. It was a slog through muddy ground, so instead I prayed. As I sat before God pouring out my heart it was as rich, powerful, and meaningful as any previous time of prayer in my life.

I prayed for everyone involved in our new church and for all the troubles I was experiencing. While lamenting and crying out in the pain and difficulty in my life, God spoke to me. He did not speak audibly, but I certainly heard him saying, "Why do you think you can handle your life?"

I responded immediately with, "You're right, I cannot."

And he spoke again very clearly, saying, "I will give you what you need for today."

One month later, my life became more unmanageable than anyone could have imagined, and the only way through was trusting God one day at a time.

———

We live fiercely independent lives, believing we can handle anything that comes our way. Moving from one accomplished task to the next, we live like we do not need anyone else. We live as though it is nice to have people around, but we do not need them. Or we believe we should be able to handle our lives, and we become despondent when we are confronted with how unmanageable our lives are.

Either way, independent or despondent, we lack the

ability to handle even the easier challenges in our lives. When something devastating comes along, we move further down these paths, becoming hardened to our own and others' humanity. Or we move to a despair that prevents us from engaging with others' hearts as well as our own. Both lead to death—relational, emotional, spiritual, and sometimes physical.

We believe and live as though we can or should be able to handle anything that comes our way. The suffering that leads to independence or despondency makes us question whether or not God is good and if we can trust him.

It is not wrong to wrestle through these doubts. Christians have not done a good job of acknowledging their doubts, and it has therefore prevented them from engaging with the pain that suffering brings. If we do not engage with doubts about God's goodness and whether we can trust him, then we will not find the truth of who God is and how he is at work in our suffering. It is only when we walk through our pain and suffering, experiencing fully their weight, that we begin to understand God's goodness in suffering.

Even though I walk through the valley of the shadow of death

This is where we live—in the valley of the shadow of death. The world is walking through the valley of the shadow of death because sin has entered the world and has cast its shadow onto all of us. The fog that surrounds our lives—the sense that something is not the way it should be—is what the Bible calls sin. What we do and know we should not can show us that there is something wrong. Even the desires within us to do what we should not seem out of place within us. And perhaps most importantly, what has been done to us shows us this world is not the way it should be. The unrest this causes in our hearts and lives is confirmed by what the Bible tells us: it is God at work in the valley of the shadow of death.

This shadow has affected the way we interact with everything. It is not just something we go through when we get the diagnosis we feared, when we lose a job with little hope of another, when a child walks away from the family, or when the love of our life dies too soon. These and other experiences are when we feel the shadow of death more intensely and see more clearly how sin and death have destroyed us, our loved ones, and this world. We see in these moments of pain that *we are all*, right now, living in this valley of the shadow of death. This psalm is about how the LORD our shepherd works in this valley.

He leads me in paths of righteousness
for his name's sake.

David twice reminds himself that God is the one leading. He writes, *"He leads me beside still waters."* And, *"He leads me in paths of righteousness."* Through the immense pain of David's life, he knows this is all God's work. David did not know what Paul would write a thousand years later in Romans 8:28: *"And we know that* for those who love God all things work together for good, for those who are called according to his purpose," but he did understand the truth there in ways we do not.

When David cries out, "O my son Absalom, my son, my son Absalom! Would I had died instead of you, O Absalom, my son, my son!" he embraces the pain of his own sin, Absalom's sin, and sin that leads to death. He simultaneously trusts that the LORD led him into this dark valley and that his sin brought him to this place.

Why is this important?

David knows he is responsible *and* this is God's sovereign will. You may have noticed that I took these last two phrases of Psalm 23 out of order. God is not just allowing sin and death to happen to us so we might turn to him and find peace. God is the one leading us in and through the sin and death in our lives. He is leading us into and through the valley of the shadow of death.

Why?

We desperately want to be led beside still waters, and we want to be free from the chaos of all which is broken in our lives and the world. Yet when he takes us into tragedy and devastation, we forget his promise to be with us in our fears. This is not just God's will; it is good. On the other side of this valley of death we will know fully God's goodness in our present darkness.

I will fear no evil, for you are with me.

I have rarely been afraid in the water. I grew up swimming competitively, and when I was sixteen, I had teammates going to the Olympic trials. I was always second best on my team, but that is a different story. Later, I lifeguarded on Virginia Beach. I have competed in ocean races and surfed twenty-foot-plus waves.

Perhaps I was too comfortable in the ocean. I did not respect it the way I needed too.

That changed in 2010 when Hurricane Earl skirted the shore of Virginia Beach. I love swimming in the ocean when there are rough seas. Swimming beyond the breakers and feeling tossed by the immense power of the waves sets me free from all the troubles on shore. I used it to escape.

I walked out on the beach on September 3 with my fins in hand looking to escape all 2010 had brought so far. As I made my way through the smaller shore break, I was taken by currents like I never had before. I was violently pulled in one direction and then another.

I swam hard for twenty minutes and saw the break in the waves which would allow me to escape into the storm-tossed sea where I could catch my breath. I knew it would take another five minutes of grueling swimming to get there. I decided to turn back and faced another twenty minutes of what became the most desperate swim of my life. I came close to losing the battle in those currents.

Moments before I got back to where I could stand, I felt my strength evaporate. I could barely get my head up to take a breath before I was pulled back down.

As a lifeguard on the same beach, I had swum out to people in much easier situations, handed them my buoy, and said, "It's going to be okay, I've got you." There was no one there to help, and I did not know how much longer I could keep swimming toward the beach. I have never been so afraid for my life.

———

It is hard for us to admit our fears. We live like we are supposed to handle all life throws our way.

- I am so afraid.
- I am afraid my wife or my children will die.
- I am afraid that I will not continue to work in my calling as a pastor.
- I am afraid we will have to move back in with our family.
- I am afraid of the guilt and shame that would come with leaving ministry again.
- I am afraid I cannot handle the next tragedy.
- I am afraid God will not be there when the next wave hits.

What are you afraid of?

I will fear no evil, for you are with me.

I need to be reminded of this promise every day. We all do. He promises to give us what we need for today. His commitment is to give us his presence.

In verse 4, David shifts from reminding himself about the promises of the LORD to reassuring himself of these promises by talking to the LORD. He is talking to God about all that has happened in his tragedy.

David's fears were realized when told of Absalom's death, and he was terribly alone.

We are alone as well.

We live like we do not need anyone, but we are also desperate to walk hand-in-hand with someone through this life, through both the joy and suffering. Yet if we have someone to share our lives with, our actions often push them away. Through all of our pain and trouble, David and God remind us that we are not alone, and our fears are met with God's perfect love.

If you do not believe God is there, or if it feels like he is far away, cry out to him now. He longs to show you his perfect love, the only thing that will cast out your fears. God promises his presence in our tragedy and trauma, and when we pray he reminds us of that promise. Pray with me now:

God, I am so afraid and so alone. I know I will not make it without you. Show me your presence in my life.

Our fears are not a failure of faith. When David writes *"I will fear no evil,"* he is not saying he has ascended to a level of faith toward which we all must strive.

We often hear a message that goes something like this: "If you only had more faith, you would not be so afraid, depressed, or grief stricken." This is wrong, and if you hear this message from anyone, well-meaning or not, do not take it to heart.

David is not saying, "I have no fear because God is

with me." This is not the biblical version of the NO FEAR bumper sticker.

Because this is poetry, we have to adjust the way we think. As Christians, we have become conditioned to read every part of the Bible the same way we read the Epistles, the letters written to the Church in the first century. What they do is teach through instruction and argument.

Poetry teaches us differently. It uses words, metaphors, and similes to get at the heart of the matter. So, when David writes, *"I will fear no evil because you are with me,"* he is communicating the same idea the Apostle John does in his first letter to the first-century church: *"There is no fear in love, but perfect love casts out fear"* (1 John 4:18).

John is more direct or is speaking more clearly. Through poetry, David connects our hearts and souls to God's presence with us even in our fears.

David is saying, "When I am afraid; when I cannot find rest; when I am desperate for something to help or fix my pain; when my soul is troubled and distressed; when this happens—I will, I can, and I need to remember I am not alone. I will remember the LORD is my shepherd, and he loves me."

I wish I could tell you that understanding this will take away all your fears. It will not, and that is not what David is communicating. In and through our fears, the LORD is our shepherd, and he is with each of us as we walk fearfully into the valley of the shadow of death.

Your rod and your staff, they comfort me.

- Comfort
- Comfort food
- Comfy shoes/sofa/sheets/bed
- Comfort zone
- Comfort Inn
- Comfort Suites
- Travel in comfort
- A comfortable feeling

The use of the word "comfort" has increased nearly 150 percent since 1980.[1] This should not be surprising. It is what we experience every day here in the United States—comfort has become an ultimate goal. I think Pink Floyd gets it right in their 1979 song "Comfortably Numb":

When I was a child
I caught a fleeting glimpse
Out of the corner of my eye
I turned to look but it was gone
I cannot put my finger on it now
The child is grown
The dream is gone
I have become comfortably numb[2]

We have grown up and found comfort and pleasure more attainable than our hopes and dreams. Even if we cannot afford the most comfortable and pleasurable, we still know they can be found each day. These numb us from pain, hurt, and hope.

Psalm 69 is attributed to David, perhaps when he was fleeing from King Saul. In this psalm, we clearly hear lament, pain, and David's cry. He is beaten down, attacked, and distressed. He writes:

Reproaches have broken my heart,
so that I am in despair
I looked for pity, but there was none,
and for comforters, but I found none. (Ps. 69:20)

David wanted comfort from others, but it was not there. He wanted to be told, "It is going to be okay. Things are not as bad as you think. There are others who suffer worse than you do. You should just get over it and move on."

We often hear these platitudes from well-meaning friends and family who try to help. It was God's grace to David that he did not receive any of those lesser comforts.

They are what Job called "empty nothings." Job suffered tragedy upon tragedy, and his so-called friends' help was anything but. We read: *"How then will you comfort me with empty nothings? There is nothing left of your answers but falsehood"* (Job 21:34). We pursue these empty nothings with reckless abandon. These comforts will not provide; nor will they last. But we still seek them.

Have you heard of Joseph and how his brothers sold him into slavery? It is an amazing biblical story that covers forty years of how God redeems one family. You can find this story of hope in Genesis 37 and 39–50.

Joseph's brothers told their father Jacob that Joseph had been killed, and this was Jacob's response:

> *All his sons and all his daughters rose up to comfort him, but he refused to be comforted and said, "No, I shall go down to Sheol to my son, mourning." Thus his father wept for him.* (Gen. 37:35)

Jacob refused to be comforted because grief and mourning are more important in such times than comforts. These comforts, and the way in which we pursue them, do not provide what we so desperately need.

Grief and mourning can actually take us to true comfort.

In his book *Counterfeit Gods*, Tim Keller identifies comfort as one of four "deep idols." The others are power, approval, and control. Keller describes these deep or core idols as "our basic motivational drives."[3] They dictate what we do and what we value. We value comfort above all else because it is a way to avoid and escape. It is far and away from true comfort. God speaks in the Bible about true comfort, the comfort only he provides:

> *Comfort, comfort my people, says your God.*
> *Speak tenderly to Jerusalem,*

and cry to her
that her warfare is ended,
that her iniquity is pardoned,
that she has received from the LORD's hand
double for all her sins. (Isa. 40:1–2)

Sitting by a fire in your favorite chair while the snow comes down outside is not God's comfort. Crawling into a warm bed with your partner at the end of a long day is not how God comforts his people. A stack of pancakes fresh off the griddle with a heap of butter and warm maple syrup is not the comfort God promises to provide.

These comforts are good gifts from God, and they can point us to what is true and right. They are at best the means but not the end. It is only in the end, on the other side of the valley, that we find true and complete comfort. The comfort of God is the one who knows all we have done and who knows all that has been done to us and still delights to call us his own. The comfort of the LORD is he who has and will redeem every sin and who is at work making all things right again. He will take what is broken and make it more beautiful than if it had never crashed to the floor. The comfort of God is leading us to the other side of the valley of the shadow of death. It is this comfort David had in view when writing Psalm 23.

Your rod and your staff, they comfort me.

The rod here is used for disciplining and protection.

Perhaps you have heard the phrase, "spare the rod and spoil the child." It has been used by Christians to defend spanking their children. Its closest reference in the Bible is Proverbs 13:24: *"Whoever spares the rod hates his son, but he who loves him is diligent to discipline him."* There is no mention of "spoil the child" in the Bible but many make that assumption.

I do not intend to engage in the conversation on the use of physical discipline. I want to lead us to a fully biblical understanding of what is meant by the word "rod" in Psalm 23 and in other places in Scripture. It is a reference to discipline, but not all discipline is physical. Protection is an equally important concept of "rod" to understand alongside discipline. Perhaps we have over-emphasized discipline and neglected protection.

David is referencing the gentle care and protection of a shepherd here. Before becoming king, that was his job. He was a shepherd. When David announced to Saul, the king of Israel at the time, that he would fight Goliath, he made it clear he knew how a shepherd used the rod:

David said to Saul, *"Your servant used to keep sheep for his father. And when there came a lion, or a bear, and took a lamb from the flock, I went after him and struck him and delivered it out of his mouth. And if he arose against me, I caught him by his beard and struck him and killed him.* (1 Sam. 17:34–35)

A smack on a sheep's hindquarters to keep it from

going in the wrong direction is an important part of shepherding, but the dangers for the sheep do not just come from within. Perhaps we have ignored the dangers outside because our individualistic American Church culture has focused mainly on our personal sin issues. I do not want to make any less of the dangers of sin in our lives, the ways in which our longings lead us away from the Good Shepherd. I want us to understand more clearly that our Shepherd is actively protecting us from evil, from those who want us to run from the tender care of the Shepherd. The LORD protects his people from spiritual evil in ways we will never see or know. The Apostle Peter writes:

> Humble yourselves, therefore, under the mighty hand of God so that at the proper time he may exalt you, casting all your anxieties on him, because he cares for you. Be sober-minded; be watchful. Your adversary the devil prowls around like a roaring lion, seeking someone to devour. (1 Pet. 5:6–8)

We need to be sober-minded, and we need to be watchful, but more importantly we need to be reminded that he cares for us. His comfort protects us from danger from without as well as within. We all know and long for the comfort of security, whether it is physical or emotional. And we all know the fear and anxiety that comes when aspects of our lives are insecure. David knows from experience as a shepherd that the comfort God provides is being able to rest and lie down in security.

You prepare a table before me.

Do you remember the best food you have tasted?

My friend Allen Routt is the chef and owner of The Painted Lady in Newberg, Oregon. The gnocchi and pork belly Allen prepared when I visited were outstanding. A great meal though is not just the food on the table. The people you are with at the table is what makes it amazing.

Asaph was a contemporary of David. In Psalm 78, Asaph writes about God's people in the wilderness after fleeing Egypt. To describe their ongoing complaints, he uses the language we find in Psalm 23:

> *Yet they sinned still more against him,*
> *Rebelling against the Most High in the desert.*
> *They tested God in their heart*
> *by demanding the food they craved.*
> *They spoke against God, saying,*
> *"Can God spread a table in the wilderness?"*
> (Ps. 78:17–19)

The answer to their question is an emphatic yes. The LORD himself prepares and hosts this table. On Sundays, I stand behind this same table inviting those who place their trust in Jesus to come participate in the sacrament of the Lord's Supper.

This table and the one David references in Psalm 23 invite us to stop striving to make our lives work or to stop despairing because our lives are not working. The table is an invitation to rest and trust in Jesus, the Good

Shepherd. He leads us beside still waters. He makes us lie down and rest. He invites us to his table, and this is no simple fare—the table here represents the feast to come at the wedding supper of the Lamb. It is described here in the book of Revelation:

> Then I heard what seemed to be the voice of a great
> multitude, like the roar of many waters and like the
> sound of mighty peals of thunder, crying out,
> "Hallelujah!
> For the Lord our God
> the Almighty reigns.
> Let us rejoice and exult
> and give him the glory,
> for the marriage of the Lamb has come,
> and his Bride has made herself ready;
> it was granted her to clothe herself
> with fine linen, bright and pure"
> for the fine linen is the righteous deeds of the saints.
> And the angel said to me, "Write this: Blessed are those
> who are invited to the marriage supper of the Lamb."
> And he said to me, "These are the true words of God."
> (Rev. 19:6–9)

When my wife Robin and I were engaged and planning our wedding, she was content to have family and a few close friends. I had just turned forty, had two kids from a previous marriage, and she was just a year younger. The conventional wisdom for that stage of life is a small wedding.

But I had other plans, and they were because of this passage from Revelation.

I wanted our wedding to be a taste of the wedding feast to come. I planned the service to echo the redemption Robin and I had experienced through Jesus and in our relationship. We invited everyone who was there to the table of the Lord's Supper, the meal of our Redeemer. We hoped whoever wanted to come would be there celebrating with us, so we invited more than one thousand guests and at least three hundred of them joined us. There was a party with a live band and a feast with beer and wine. We celebrated what God had done in our relationship, what he was doing in our lives, and what he would do in our marriage. My hope was for everyone to experience in a small part what we all will experience when Jesus returns and takes us to the party that all parties hope to become—the best food, the best drink, the best company—the table for which we were made. We had a foretaste of that table of abundance, peace, and rest because of Jesus' work.

The LORD prepares this table for us right now. Psalm 23 points to Jesus' table. It is prepared for each of us in the presence of all our enemies and most importantly, in the presence of our enemies sin and death.

You prepare a table before me in the presence of my enemies.

Who are your enemies?
Does someone specific come to mind?

Someone who has wronged you in deep and painful ways?

Someone you cannot seem to forgive or refuse to forgive?

I understand. I have felt that pain and know how impossible it is to forgive someone who has hurt you deeply. I will not tell you here how to move forward in forgiveness or say your pain and fears are not legitimate. I am not saying we forget our anger. Not all anger is wrong.

With our pain, our hurt, and our anger, there is a deeper enemy. This does not negate the pain and hurt caused by the person we call an enemy. The deeper enemy is death at work in our pain. The reason it hurts so deeply is because it is in fact death. It is not the way the most beautiful part of creation is to be treated. That person we call our enemy has brought death into our lives.

Perhaps you believe you are your own worst enemy. You see how your actions have brought death into your life and in others' lives. It is right and good to mourn these actions and to turn away from living as you have been, seeking your own desires rather than serving and caring for others. It is important to seek and pursue forgiveness and reconciliation. Just as with those who have been wronged and for those who have wronged others, the enemy is death and sin. Death and sin are one and the same. There is no sin without death and no death without sin. It is the first and last enemy. Paul writes:

For as by a man came death, by a man has come also the resurrection of the dead. For as in Adam all die, so also in Christ shall all be made alive. But each in his own order: Christ the first fruits, then at his coming those who belong to Christ. Then comes the end, when he delivers the kingdom to God the Father after destroying every rule and every authority and power. For he must reign until he has put all his enemies under his feet. The last enemy to be destroyed is death. (1 Cor. 15:21–26)

The LORD prepares this table in the presence of sin and death. This table is the promise of an end to sin and death. This promise is given while we suffer under the tyranny of sin and death's rule. "How can a good God allow suffering?" is not answered fully here. The table contains the promise of the answer and gives hope as we wait for that promise to be fulfilled.

You prepare a table before me in the presence of my enemies; you anoint my head with oil; my cup overflows.

This table promises redemption, forgiveness, and reconciliation with others. This reconciliation is with those we call enemies, and more importantly it is reconciliation with God. Sin—our own and others—pulls us away from the Good Shepherd. So when David says that the LORD anoints his head with oil, it means God sets him apart, makes him holy, and calls him back to the Shepherd. For David and for us, God does this in the presence of our enemies sin and death. It is here and now that our cups overflow as God gives us more than we will ever need. We cannot rise up against these enemies. We cannot fight death. That work is God's alone. It is the work of the Good Shepherd. While God is at work, he invites us to feast and to rest. He restores us to himself. He makes us his own. He gives us more than we will ever need. He does this while we are in the valley of the shadow of death. This is the hope for today. This is the hope for right now.

Questions for Further Reflection and Study

- Where are you walking today that feels like death?

- When have you felt the most alone? How does that shape the way you interact with God?

- When have you felt the most comfort from someone?

- How can this inform the way you consider God's presence in your life?

- Meditate on YHWY honoring you and welcoming you right now to his banquet.

HOW CAN WE SUFFER WITH HOPE?

God's promises as he leads us through the valley of death and suffering are incomprehensible. He shows us contentment: *"I shall not want."* While death surrounds us, he promises rest: *"He leads me beside still waters."* When our hearts, minds, and bodies are broken: *"He restores my soul."* He gives us more than restoration. He promises us his presence—to be with us as we walk through the valley of shadow. Even during our worst pain and suffering, he gives us the assurance we can walk without fear. He promises comfort, protection, growth, a feast, and more. This is a future promise and a promise for right now while we are walking through the valley. The comfort of a feast is in the presence of our enemies, comfort when we come face to face with the ultimate enemy, the last enemy—death. And when restoration is complete, our lives will not just be restored. They will be better than before our pain and suffering.

After leaving Seattle and closing the new church I

had started, I worked several different jobs trying to discern my new calling and if vocational ministry was still what God had for me. The best job was at Trader Joe's. If you are going to work at a grocery store, work for Trader Joe's. Customer service is the highest priority, and they create this culture through building a fun, encouraging, and welcoming team dynamic.

I quickly developed wonderful friendships there. As they got to know me and I them it became clear to my TJ's family that we cared for each other. There were only a couple of Christians on the team but everyone knew I was theirs and they were mine. I did not hide that I was an ordained Presbyterian minister without a church, and no one took issue with what I believed, not the decidedly atheist, the agnostic, the pseudo Buddhist, or even the practicing witch. In fact, it led to many questions on their part and fantastic discussions without any antagonism, fear, or anger. I loved them, and they loved me.

One of those conversations was with a guy I will call Jeff. He was a recent college graduate, and I was twenty years older. He was an atheist and wanted to know how I could square Christianity and science. The conversation was not heated but perhaps a little intense. This happened while we were stocking the cereal aisle after the store had closed, lots and lots of Joe's O's. There were six to eight others listening in. At ten o'clock at night, with loud upbeat music playing all throughout the store, we talked about evolution, the scientific method, the nature of faith, free will, God's sovereignty, Jesus, redemption, forgiveness, and the problem of suffering. It was a long conversation and made putting up all those boxes of Joe's O's go by quickly.

Jeff finally asked, "Why would God create a system that would allow for sin and death?" Of course, there was more behind his questions about science and faith. I stopped stocking, looked at him directly with all the love and respect which had grown between us and our TJ's family, and said, "Because redemption is far more beautiful than perfection."

Jeff stopped talking for a minute, which was unusual for him. He said, "I think you just converted me."

I was not trying to. I wanted to love him well, answer his questions, and share how I had seen the beauty of redemption. When we are on the other side of the valley and the work of redemption is complete, our lives will be more beautiful than if we had never suffered pain, trauma, and death. Redemption is beautiful.

Sometimes the valley seems pitch-black. It seems too dark to see the light. Have you ever been in a canyon where you can only catch a glimpse of the sky? There are more canyons here in Montana than anywhere else I have lived. The canyons appear deep and dark. The same thing can happen downtown in a big city because of the skyscrapers. We see there is sun, but it is not shining on us. This is often our experience during deep pain.

———

While I was starting a new church in Seattle, I became the pastor I never thought I would be. I lost sight of what was going on with my family. It happened because of the intense pressure of starting a new church and ministry, particularly with the church that brought me out to begin this new work. There was so much going on around me, all I thought about and did was ministry.

I never thought that would be me because "those guys" were arrogant, Type A, hard-charging, and all about themselves. I struggle with pride and arrogance like anyone, but I did not see what was happening around me. I lost sight of what was going on with my family, and I wanted my ex-wife to be okay.

I thought she was okay, but I did not really ask.

She was not okay. To deal with her pain, she sought the arms of another man.

When she left, it was devastating.

That day, before I knew what happened, I called our counselor to discuss a ministry-related issue. It quickly became clear to me there was something bigger going on. Our counselor said to me, "This will be a very hard night for you."

In that moment, I saw clearly what had been going on with my ex-wife through the past few months. She and another man had been cultivating an adulterous relationship. It is often true that when people finally discover their spouse's affair, they realize they missed all the signs that were there. I knew who it was. I knew how it had happened. And I had missed it for months.

Later that evening, after getting the kids home from school and arranging someone to sit with them, I sat in the senior pastor's office with him and with my counselor on speaker phone. She read to me an email my ex-wife had sent to her but had addressed to me.

It was devastating. It was the worst moment of my life. The sound that escaped from me was guttural. It was more than wailing, more than hurt and pain. It was death coming out of my soul as noise. It was my greatest fear coming true: to be fully known and rejected.

That was the darkest part of the valley I have ever walked through, and I walked through it for two years.

There have been times when God's Word has come into my life and been illuminated by the Holy Spirit. He has shown me truths in the Bible I had not seen before even after previously reading the same passage multiple times. He has shown me his goodness in ways I had not yet experienced.

When this happens, I get excited to share the good news I have experienced through the Holy Spirit. What the Holy Spirit did with Psalm 23 in the months that followed my ex-wife's departure was different. It kept despair from turning to suicide. Without Psalm 23 I may well have stepped out my door and walked the mile and half to the 99 bridge over the canal. That was the plan, 150 feet to end it all.

In the darkest night of my soul, I had Psalm 23. Because I had drilled it into my brain not even two years prior, it was there to move into my heart and soul. There were many sleepless nights because of the pain and trauma. However, in the midst of the pain I repeated *"The Lord is my shepherd. I shall not want"* again and again. There were nights I drifted off to sleep while praying Psalm 23. There were nights when sleep did not come, and I tried to turn to malignancies like pornography and alcohol in hopes the pain would go away. Thankfully, God did not allow me to escape. The deep wounds remained obvious, and God spared me further devastation from those malignancies.

One day when the kids were in school, I decided to go see a movie. I wanted to escape into one of my favorite benign pursuits. This was 2010, and Denzel Washington's movie *The Book of Eli* had just come out. The story is of a post-apocalyptic United States, and it centers on Denzel's character, Eli, fighting his way across the country for reasons we do not understand at first. As the story progresses, we learn Eli has the last copy of the Bible, and he is trying to get it to a safe place. At one point, he is hiding in a cave with another character. She asks him to read something from the Bible, and he starts reciting Psalm 23.

I had been praying those words every night for the past three weeks. I started weeping in the theater. I could not hold back the audible sobs. Thankfully, there were only a handful of others there in the middle of the day.

I wanted to escape. I wanted to run away. I wanted to run away from all the pain and to something that could make me comfortably numb. I did not want to deal with the trauma. God did not let me run. He said, "No. You need to remember right now in this pain that I am your shepherd, and with me you will not want. You need not fear evil, and I am with you always."

Surely goodness and mercy shall follow me
all the days of my life.

Let's look at the key words in this phrase.

Surely—As noted above, most translation decisions are based on our understanding of the original languages and some on how familiar people are with the wording. People have been reciting this verse in Psalm 23 in English essentially the same way since the King James Version was first published in 1611. "Surely" can also be translated as "only." The same word is translated as "only" in other places throughout the Old Testament.

Translating it as "surely" is not wrong, but with translation, there is always more to gain by considering other legitimate options. "Only" communicates the truth of God working for our good even through suffering.

Goodness—In the Hebrew, this word is simply "good." In the very first chapter of the Bible when we read the account of creation, God sees what he has made and says it is good. It is the exact same word used here in verse 6. In English, "goodness" is the noun form of the adjective "good," and the distinction between the two in Hebrew is not significant.

The goodness in Psalm 23 is the good in Genesis 1. Six times in the first chapter of the Bible, God says his creation is good, and this was before sin and death existed, before they had darkened the world with their stain, before there was *"the valley of the shadow of death."* It was not until after he had created man and woman that he looked out at the beauty of this world and of humankind that he says "very good."

It is all very good. The sunset on a cold day with a few clouds lit up with pink, purple, yellow, and orange is beautiful—it is very good. The blue sky dotted with puffy white clouds over the beach and ocean as the wind blows the spray off the waves back out to sea—beautiful, very good. Rolling hills with their trees at the peak of their fall colors in golden brown, yellow, orange, and red—magnificent, beautiful, very good. A newborn stretching out for the first time and breathing her first breath—amazing, unimaginably beautiful, very good. People, with brown skin, dark brown, and black skin, light brown, lighter brown, pale and pink, tints of yellow or red—all very good. Golden hair, jet-black hair, deep to light orange, brown of every shade—very good. Brown eyes flecked with gold, the deepest green or blue eyes to palest green and gray-blue, black like the night with the shine of the stars peeking out—very good. Every shade of skin, hair, and eyes, every size, every shape, every nose, every chin, every part created by God is beautiful, glorious, and radiant. Words cannot fully express your beauty. The pinnacle of God's creation. You. Very Good.

Sin, death, pain, trauma, and suffering have put a dark cloud over God's beautiful creation. It has spread a fog over the world and over our hearts that obscures our view of what is good and right. This makes it so what is good and right is not seen clearly. It has put us all on this path through *the valley of the shadow of death,*" but it has not unmade the foundation God created, named, and said is very good. There is still this fog of sin, death, pain, and suffering, but it cannot completely block out the light. And despite the shadow and the dark clouds, we still see beauty and goodness.

We are what is beautiful and very good. We are broken, and we will be until we are on the other side of the valley, but our sin and how we have been sinned against does not destroy God's beauty in us. You are being pursued right now by all the very good of our LORD.

Mercy —The Hebrew word translated here as "mercy" is a form of the word that is translated throughout the Old Testament as "steadfast love," *hesed*. *Hesed* is God's love for his people. It is the Good Shepherd's love for his flock. *Hesed* has so much more in view than just steadfast love. It is more than loving-kindness, more than unconditional love, and more than mercy or grace. It is all of those and more. My favorite definition is from Sally Lloyd-Jones' *The Jesus Storybook Bible,* which we should all read whether we have children or not. It says God's love is "Never-Stopping, Never Giving Up, Unbreaking, Always and Forever.[1] This love pursues us today.

Follows—This word probably should be translated "pursues." When I go on a hike with my dog, he follows behind. Sometimes he is right on my heels, and other times he is following from a much greater distance. Sometimes I lose sight of him, but because he is so codependent, he is never far away.

Not long after my ex-wife left, a well-meaning friend said it probably did not feel like God's goodness and mercy were following very closely. This did not sit with me well, but he had loved and cared for me through that devastation, so I did not say anything at the time. I also could not quite put my finger on why it did not seem like the right sentiment. "Follow" is not a bad word choice in English, but "pursues" is far better. God is good, and his Never-Stopping, Never Giving Up, Unbreaking, Always and Forever Love is not just following behind with hopes we will remember he is there.

The LORD is *pursuing* each of us. Each of us is chased down. Each of us hunted. Each of us pursued all the days of our lives.

Every single day.

In our darkest moments, in the deepest and darkest part of the valley, every single day. The steadfast love of the LORD pursues us.

Do you trust that the LORD is good? How are you defining "good" and "trust"? Often we try to understand God and his character by our experiences. This happens when starting from our understanding to try and make sense of God. We have to begin the work of understanding God from what he says about himself. If we define "good" and "trust" by our experiences, we will not trust God is good. God never promises our experiences will feel good.

And I shall dwell in the house of the LORD
forever.

I have lived in eighteen different places I have called home.

That is too many. Nobody likes moving. I love adventure and living in new places, but it takes its toll. My wife lived in the same house until she graduated from college, but I never had a place that was *the* family home. After my father died tragically when I was eighteen and my mother and sister moved to a different state, I was adrift. I felt homeless.

As I struggle to find my home, Jesus' words to his disciples in the upper room discourse are a balm to my soul. The Apostle John writes: *"Jesus answered him, 'If anyone loves me, he will keep my word, and my Father will love him, and we will come to him and make our home with him'"* (John 14:23).

I want this world to be my home. I would like the security of living in the same house for years to come. About a year ago, my wife and I purchased a home, and we dream of living here for years to come. I want that security for my wife and my children—a place they can call home. A place where they will say, "This is where I grew up." My older kids did not have that and neither did I. In the eight years we have been married, my wife and I have lived in five different homes. It has created a longing for me, my wife, and my children that I know will not be satisfied until we are on the other side of this valley.

Yet I have found my home. Or rather, Jesus called me into his. When God shares with us his name, he is inviting us into the intimacy shared between the Father, Son, and Spirit. In this intimacy we find security. This calling to share intimacy and find security comes to us. He gives a certainty of peace that we will never find in the buildings and places we have lived. Our houses here in the valley cannot satisfy our longings. At the moment he calls us to himself, we are dwelling in his house. We live in this promise while we walk through the valley today.

In the Hebrew, there are two words that are translated as "forever." The first one, *lorek*, refers to a long length, often used as an expression of time. The second is *yamim*. It is a form of the word day, and in this case it is plural. It says we will dwell in the house of the LORD for a long time, which, given the word construction, communicates the idea of forever. In Psalm 21:4, David uses a similar construction translated "length of days." He writes, *"He asked life of you; you gave it to him, length of days forever and ever."* But in Psalm 21, David adds two different words that are translated "forever and ever" which we do not find in Psalm 23:6. In Psalm 93, unattributed but possibly David's, the same phrase *lorek yamim* is used and translated "forevermore." We read: *"Your decrees are very trustworthy; holiness befits your house, O LORD, forevermore"* (Ps. 93:5). The New International Version (NIV) translates this phrase in Psalm 93:5 as "for endless days." The NIV for this phrase in 21:4 says "length of days." The NIV for Psalm 23:6 reads "forever" just as the English Standard Version (ESV) does.

We need to remember that this is poetry. Poetry uses words and phrases differently than other genres. Poetry engages and activates our hearts and souls to communicate in such a way that informs our innermost being as well as our minds. At times I will translate verses and passages myself using the tools from my graduate studies in Hebrew and Greek. The way I translate this poetic phrase is "always and forever." I would translate this verse: "Only God's good and steadfast love will pursue me all the days of my life and I will dwell in the house of YHWY always and forever."

The phrase "all the days of my life" tells us these promises are true for us in the thick of the fog of sin and death that lay heavy upon this valley. The phrase "dwell in the house of YHWY" tells us these promises are true for us for an eternity where we will rest with our souls restored. We have hope today, not only because of what comes on the other side of the valley with our Good Shepherd, but because he is the one leading us through this valley of the shadow of death. He leads us, and when we go astray or have been led astray, he pursues us with his Never-Stopping, Never Giving Up, Unbreaking, Always and Forever Love.

Questions for Further Reflection and Study

- What is the difference between being pursued by goodness and mercy rather than followed?

- What in this psalm can help on the days when God's goodness and mercy seem far away?

- Is this only a future hope?

- How do we experience the realities of God's house today?

- What are the real-world promises of a forever with God found in Psalm 23?

THE GOOD SHEPHERD

We have been working our way toward our Good Shepherd. We cannot fully understand YHWY as our Shepherd without considering Jesus. YHWY is one God in three persons—Father, Son, and Spirit. The way he has made himself known to us is through Jesus.

The metaphor of sheep and shepherd comes to us over and over again throughout the Bible. The first task given to Adam by God was to name every living creature (Gen. 2:20). This is the beginning of a shepherd's care. Adam and Eve's second son Abel was a keeper of sheep (Gen. 4:2). Noah was charged with the care of every living creature (Gen. 6:19). Further in Genesis we read the stories of Abraham, Isaac, Jacob, and Joseph who all labored as shepherds of sheep. As Jacob was dying he asked *"the God who has been my shepherd all my life long to this day"* to bless his son Joseph's boys (Gen. 48:15).

Moses worked as a shepherd for forty years before God used him to rescue his people from slavery in Egypt

(Exod. 7:7). When Joshua took the mantle of leadership from Moses, we learned he was the shepherd of God's people:

> *Let the LORD, the God of the spirits of all flesh, appoint a man over the congregation who shall go out before them and come in before them, who shall lead them out and bring them in, that the congregation of the LORD may not be as sheep that have no shepherd.* (Num. 27:16–17)

Saul was appointed as shepherd over Israel (2 Sam. 5:2). When David was anointed as king, God made the connection between his work as a shepherd of sheep and his role leading the people of God:

> *In all places where I have moved with all the people of Israel, did I speak a word with any of the judges of Israel, whom I commanded to shepherd my people Israel, saying, "Why have you not built me a house of cedar?" Now, therefore, thus you shall say to my servant David, "Thus says the LORD of hosts, I took you from the pasture, from following the sheep, that you should be prince over my people Israel."* (2 Sam. 7:7–8)

The description of David's anointing as king in 1 Chronicles 11:1–3 makes his calling as a shepherd of God's people clear:

> *And the LORD your God said to (David), "You shall be shepherd of my people Israel, and you shall be prince over my people Israel."*

When Solomon died in 930 BC, the united Kingdom of Israel under Saul, David, and Solomon was split in two. The northern kingdom of Israel suffered under kings who served their own needs rather than protecting and providing for their people. From this point forward, we begin to hear prophecies against the shepherds who did not fulfill their callings. Eighty years after the Kingdom of God was divided, the prophet Micaiah spoke the word of the LORD against one of the evil kings in the North, Ahab: *"And he said, 'I saw all Israel scattered on the mountains, as sheep that have no shepherd'"* (1 Kings 22:17). As a king, Ahab was called to care for his people. Instead, he sought power and conquest. Some 700 years prior to Jesus' birth, the prophet Isaiah wrote this about the coming messiah:

> *He will tend his flock like a shepherd;*
> *he will gather the lambs in his arms;*
> *he will carry them in his bosom,*
> *and gently lead those that are with young.*
> (Isa. 40:11)

The prophet Jeremiah gives us hope for shepherds after God's own heart who will lead us in knowledge and understanding (Jer. 3:15). Jeremiah also identifies himself as one of those good shepherds (Jer. 17:15). This prophet spends most of his time speaking against the shepherds who serve themselves, even calling them stupid (Jer. 10:21), and further invectives are found throughout the rest of the book. But he does give us hope for good shepherds:

Then I will gather the remnant of my flock out of all the countries where I have driven them, and I will bring them back to their fold, and they shall be fruitful and multiply. I will set shepherds over them who will care for them, and they shall fear no more, nor be dismayed, neither shall any be missing, declares the LORD. (Jer. 23:3–4)

Ezekiel also was charged by God to prophesy against the shepherds of Israel for using people to serve their own desires. These shepherds were the leaders and the priests of God's people prior to the Babylonian exile. This abuse of power and predatory behavior is rightly deserving of God's wrath. We read:

The word of the LORD came to me: "Son of man, prophesy against the shepherds of Israel; prophesy, and say to them, even to the shepherds, Thus says the Lord GOD: Ah, shepherds of Israel who have been feeding yourselves! Should not shepherds feed the sheep? You eat the fat, you clothe yourselves with the wool, you slaughter the fat ones, but you do not feed the sheep. The weak you have not strengthened, the sick you have not healed, the injured you have not bound up, the strayed you have not brought back, the lost you have not sought, and with force and harshness you have ruled them. So they were scattered, because there was no shepherd, and they became food for all the wild beasts. My sheep were scattered; they wandered over all the mountains and on every high hill. My sheep were scattered over all the face of the earth, with none to search or seek for them." (Ezek. 34:2–6)

As one called by God to shepherd and care for his people, I tremble in fear reading this passage. Its warning is clear, and the consequences for pursuing my work with evil intent are dire. I have counseled those who have suffered spiritual abuse and neglect by pastors and church leaders and seen firsthand its devastation. I too have been crushed by shepherds who sought to serve themselves. Those who were called to care for our souls who then chose to serve themselves are held responsible for our wandering, (Hebr. 13:17). As we sing in *Come Thou Fount of Every Blessing*,[1] we are prone to wander, and we have been allowed to wander, becoming scattered and worse. I can only serve in this role as a spiritual shepherd because our Good Shepherd is at work.

In John 10:11, Jesus identifies himself as both the Good Shepherd and YHWY. In his gospel, the Apostle John records Jesus identifying himself as I AM seven different times:

- I AM the bread of life.
- I AM the light of the world.
- I AM the door of the sheep.
- I AM the good shepherd.
- I AM the resurrection and the life.
- I AM the way, the truth, and the life.
- I AM the true vine.

There is no question Jesus is identifying himself as YHWY with these statements in the same way God identified himself to Moses in the burning bush. Two of them are in John 10 and are about sheep and shepherds.

Thus, we can now understand that David was praying to Jesus when he wrote Psalm 23 even though he did not know when the Messiah King would arrive.

Jesus leads us to contentment—*I shall not want.*

Jesus makes us rest even when we do not want to or think we need to—*He makes me lie down in green pastures. He leads me beside still waters.*

Jesus gives tender care in our innermost being—*He restores my soul.*

Jesus leads us through the valley of death. He is with us, so we need not fear. He comforts and protects us. He invites us to his table of forgiveness with the promise of life. He does it right now in this valley. Jesus pursues us with steadfast love. He makes his home with us now and forevermore. Jesus accomplishes this through laying down his life for his sheep. He said, *"I am the good shepherd. The good shepherd lays down his life for the sheep"* (John 10:11).

If there were job posts for shepherds, you would not find on the list of required duties to protect the sheep at all costs even if the cost is your life. A shepherd keeps her sheep from harm, but would she give her life to do so? A shepherd will leave his flock to go after the one gone astray, but to do this at the cost of his life is unreasonable. Our Good Shepherd lays down his life for us, and the only reasons for him to do this is because it is absolutely necessary and it is a part of who he is.

The first reason he dies in our place is the character of our Good Shepherd. The metaphor breaks down at this point because we are trying to understand who this Good Shepherd is by our limited human understanding. It is going around the circle the wrong way, and we are prone to do this whenever we try to define God by our experiences rather than by who he says he is. If a circle has two points on opposite sides—one point God and the other us—when we then start trying to make sense of God and all he has done from our perspective, we will never make it to the other side. We will never understand who God is by starting with ourselves. Whatever God says about himself is where we begin, and here he says he is a shepherd that lays down his life for his sheep. This is his character of self-sacrifice. Rather than letting us suffer the consequences for our wandering, he takes them for us. Once we are his and he is ours, there is nothing we have done or will do that changes his character of self-sacrifice.

He is our shepherd, and he is good. As sheep will approach their shepherd when she is near, we have the freedom to go to Jesus at any time with our needs. When we do not or will not go to him, he chases us down, pursuing us relentlessly. He wants us to come to him. We are his and know his voice, so when he calls we go.

Do you hear him calling? Do you know his voice? You can hear it in Psalm 23.

The second reason he lays down his life for us is because otherwise we would die. Sheep die when they wander away from the flock and their shepherd. Some are torn apart by wild animals. Others die of thirst, and then they are lost and cannot find their way toward water. When sheep fall and end up on their backs, it is difficult for them to roll back to their feet. A few will suffocate and die on their backs without the help to get back up on their feet. If sheep wander for too long, their wool coats can become long and heavy, causing them to die from heat stroke.

Instead of letting us suffer these deaths, our Good Shepherd takes on death himself. Our sin is too great. How we have been sinned against is too much for us to bear. Jesus loves us too much to let us perish in sin. It is his great joy to die so we might live, so we do not have to live under the weight of sin always and forever.

Earlier, I gave different words to help us express and experience our grief. The opposite of grief is joy. Jesus knows how great our grief and suffering is, and so it is his joy to give us hope in our journey through sin and death. Even when it is too much to bear, we can find hope and joy in Jesus and what he provides for us.

The darkest part of this valley I have walked through were the two years after my former wife left. Those two years included suffering through chemotherapy and radiation because of Hodgkin's lymphoma. That diagnosis came less than a year after closing the new church in Seattle.

During that time, I learned how to suffer even when there was not anything happy in my life. I became content in suffering because I knew I was not alone, that Jesus was leading me through the pain. Rather than end it all in suicide, I learned how to walk through this valley because I loved my children and I knew there would be others whom I would be called upon to serve.

As I learned to walk with Jesus through suffering, I found joy in giving my life away for others. I did not hope for someone else to share my life with, but that is what God provided.

Robin was thirty-eight when we met, and I turned forty only eleven days after our first date. Neither of us were interested in dating for fun. We quickly shared deeply and personally about our lives. Robin's story is different from mine, but she too had learned to depend on Jesus through her own trauma and suffering.

As we shared our griefs with each other, I told her I did not want to cry any less because there is much that deserves our tears. But I wanted to laugh more.

And we did, and we do. We shared hope and joy like we never had before. Robin is a Korean-American adoptee, and we wanted our girls to have that connection to her mother's heritage and to their parents' story. God's good gifts to us abounded, and when our girls were born, we gave them middle names which are Korean for "hope" and" joy"—Gidae and Gippeum.

There are good gifts ahead for all of us even as we walk through sin and death. Hope and joy will come.

I wish I could tell you when. I wish I could fix your pain and promise you that you will not suffer anymore because of the Good Shepherd's care.

I cannot.

Yet our God is good, and we will not always walk through this desert of our souls, but that is not the promise. The promise is he walks with us through pain, trauma, suffering, grief, fear, and anxiety. He walks with us and provides comfort because he too has walked through these.

Sin and death are at work in our lives. They are responsible for our anxiety and fears. Our Good Shepherd knows these well. While Jesus walked the earth, he lived our sorrow and grief, and it was why he was headed to the cross.

Have you ever wondered why we do not have any account of Jesus laughing? I am sure he sat around the campfire with the disciples as they all laughed at something that had happened that day.

Perhaps Peter stepped in a bucket because he was not watching where he was going and leaving muddy footprints behind. Maybe it became a great nuisance. He then had to stop and remove the dirt that had caked between his toes and between his foot and sandal. It became an irritant to him on their long walk that day. He complained about it the rest of the day, and the others teased him because he was making a big deal out of a minor annoyance. When they sat down to make a fire and a meal, Peter realized it was something to laugh about rather than get mad about. James then gets up from the fire and imitated how Peter walked with his muddy foot, shaking it to try to get the mud out every few steps, and they all laughed.

Did Jesus laugh with them? Was there something underneath his laughter that kept him from fully entering into their merriment?

The prophet Isaiah tells us Jesus was *"a man of sorrows acquainted with grief"* (Isa. 53:3). Did Jesus understand as a child that this world's sorrow and grief would lead him to the cross? At the age of 12 Jesus sat with the scholars of the temple who *"were amazed at his understanding and his answers"* (Luke 2:47). Did he know then that he was walking toward his death? He certainly did as his ministry began. In the second chapter of John's gospel, we find the story of Jesus turning water into wine. His mother asked him to do something about the lack of wine at the wedding feast. Jesus responded, *"My hour has not yet come"* (John 2:4). That hour was the hour of his death.

In December 2010, I was diagnosed with Hodgkin's lymphoma, a cancer of the immune system. My first chemotherapy treatment was scheduled two months later. Hodgkin's Lymphoma is treatable and curable even at later stages (mine was stage 1). The prognosis was clear. I would not have to deal with it for long, and it was highly unlikely that I would die. But I knew chemotherapy would be awful, and I would feel sicker than I ever had. It would take a toll on my body, and the treatment and recovery would last for months. On the day I received the diagnosis, a new and heavy anxiety entered my life. I walked the two months toward my first treatment with these fears wrapped around my heart and soul.

As Jesus' ministry began, he knew he was walking toward something far worse than chemotherapy and even worse than death. Because he is both God and Man, he faced sin and death from the moment of his birth like he had not for the eternity prior. He walked feeling the weight of sin and death throughout his earthly life. But the death he walked toward was what we as Christians will never face. This passage is moments before his arrest. Matthew writes:

> *Then Jesus went with them to a place called Gethsemane, and he said to his disciples, "Sit here, while I go over there and pray." And taking with him Peter and the two sons of Zebedee, he began to be sorrowful and troubled. Then he said to them, "My soul is very sorrowful, even to death; remain here, and watch with me." And going a little farther he fell on his face and prayed, saying, "My Father, if it be possible, let this cup pass from me; nevertheless, not as I will, but as you will."* (Matt. 26:36–39)

Has your soul been sorrowful even to the point of death? Mine has. If you have ever had the thought that you no longer want to live in this pain and grief, then you have been there too.

———

As an important aside, if your thoughts about no longer wanting to live here in this valley of death have progressed from discouragement to despair, please stop reading and talk with someone immediately. Pick up the phone and call a friend or the National Suicide Prevention Lifeline 800-273-8255. Just the act of making that call and actually talking, not just texting, with another person will help tremendously. I know because I have been there. I have done this. Jesus was there too—anxious and fearful, even unto death. He took friends with him to the garden, and he reached out to his Father. It is never wrong to reach out to someone.

————

Anxiety, fear, distress, angst—there are many ways to express what comes with our experience of life in the valley of death. I have written about the importance of feeling and expressing our fear and anxiety even if it hurts. It is only when we are honest that we will know the power of the presence of the LORD in our lives.

Some tell us if we were stronger or if we believed the right things, then we would not experience anxiety. They are wrong.

If anxiety, fear, distress, and angst are always because of sin, then why did Jesus experience them? It is true that our sinful actions may be what is producing our anxiety. But if our anxiety is about the suffering to come because we are walking through this valley of death, then we are right to be troubled.

We cannot handle death. Jesus was walking toward death and was sorrowful and troubled. C. S. Lewis addresses the poor theology of calling all anxiety sin. He wrote:

Some people feel guilty about their anxieties and regard them as a defect of faith. I don't agree at all. They are afflictions, not sins. Like all afflictions, they are, if we can so take them, our share in the Passion of Christ.[2]

Jesus' anxiety helps us in three ways. First, we learn not every fear or sorrow is sin. We are right to be sorrowful even unto death as we walk through chemotherapy or as someone we love suffers through it. We are right to be greatly troubled when a marriage comes to an end. We should be distressed when we are not sure how we will provide for our family. We must be greatly troubled and upset by the betrayal of those who were supposed to care for us. We are right to be in agony over a loved one's death.

Second, Jesus' anxiety reminds us if we have placed our faith, hope, and trust in this Good Shepherd, then we will never face the pain he did. The abuse his body received from his arrest until the moment of his death was horrific. Few of us will ever know even a little of that physical pain.

But what came after his death is what caused him to be greatly troubled, distressed, in spiritual agony, and sorrowful unto death. It is what led him to say on the cross at the moment of his death, *"My God, my God, why have you forsaken me?"* (Matt. 27:46). He feared separation from the intimacy he had shared with the Father and Spirit for eternity. He knew the resurrection was coming, yet he, in agony, sweat drops of blood as he prayed, asking God to remove this cup of death and separation. If Yahweh Elohe—the LORD God, I AM— has come to you and made his home with you, then you are not alone through this valley of the shadow of death. He will always be with you.

Finally, Jesus' anxiety shows us how we will live through suffering. Jesus says, *"Not as I will, but as you will"* (Luke 22:42). We must recognize how bad it is AND recognize what THE Good Shepherd has promised us. It is only then that we can say, "LORD, this is awful, and I want you to take it away because I cannot handle it, but I will trust you even if this pain lasts until we are on the other side of the valley."

I want to tell you that if you prayed that prayer, then your anxiety would go away. It might, but it more than likely will not. We are not using God to fix our anxiety. We are trusting him, feeling all anxiety's crushing weight, as we wait for him to lead us to green pastures and still waters where we will find our souls restored.

Pray with me:

> *The LORD is my shepherd; I have all I need.*
> *He makes me lie down in green pastures.*
> *He leads me beside still waters.*
> *He restores my soul.*
> *He leads me in paths of righteousness*
> *for his name's sake.*
> *Even though I walk through*
> *the valley of the shadow of death,*
> *I will fear no evil,*
> *for you are with me;*
> *your rod and your staff,*
> *they comfort me.*
> *You prepare a table before me*
> *in the presence of my enemies;*

you anoint my head with oil;
my cup overflows.
Only God's good and steadfast love shall pursue me
all the days of my life,
and I shall dwell in the house of the LORD
always and forever.

CONCLUSION

Dr. Robert G. Rayburn was the founding president of Covenant Theological Seminary, and he served in that role from 1956 to 1977. One of the Dr. Rayburn stories that has been passed down to students is about what he said to prospective pastors in preaching classes after they finished a sermon. The way I heard it, he would stand or sit in the back of the room with his arms crossed with a less than encouraging look on his face. The nervous young aspiring preachers delivered one of their first sermons. After they finished, he would often remark, "Preacher, what do you want me to DO?"

It seems like a word about what we do now after this study of the heart of Psalm 23 is in order. Before that, I will speak to what may have already happened while you read and thank you for giving this little book your time.

In the introduction, I wrote that I wanted this book to draw you into the heart of Psalm 23 and closer to the Good Shepherd. Did this happen for you? If it did, then the takeaway from your time here is that experience. If you hear the Good News of Jesus our Good Shepherd from the Bible, a book, an article, a song, or in a sermon, then it has accomplished its purpose. We need to hear this Good News every day and several times a day. The good news is we do not walk alone through the valley.

Here is a way to continue to make Psalm 23 a part of how we remember Jesus the Good Shepherd in the valley. First, I will walk us through how I did this as I went through chemotherapy. Then, I will provide a template for you to do the same.

The LORD Jesus is my shepherd.
Even though I am physically spent as poison is pumped into my body, I know you are with me, Jesus. I know you are as close as any friend, maybe closer since I am all alone in this.

I have all I need.
You have given me all I need to get through this. You have provided for me in ways I could not have expected. Thank you for sending your people to provide, help, and care for me and my children through this. There is not anything I need that I do not have. Help me believe this is true.

You make me lie down in green pastures. You lead me beside still waters. You restore my soul.
Oh Jesus, could it really be you who is leading me into this pain? My body is spent, and I cannot find the rest I

want. I lay down to sleep, it does not come, and I hurt. Is there rest in you that is not physical? Will you give my soul rest even though there are months of sickness ahead? Help me believe this is what you promise to provide. This is why, like David, I can say *I shall not want*.

You lead me through paths of righteousness for your name's sake. I do not want to walk these paths. Why are you leading me this way? It hurts so much. Can I trust you through this darkness? Is this really the only path with you? I want to pray like you did in the garden. I want to trust you in my anxiety. I need you for that to happen.

Even though I walk through the valley of the shadow of death, I will fear no evil because you are with me.
I did not know it could be this dark. Forgive me for ignoring for so long the serious nature of sin and death in my life. I know I have to go down this path, but I am scared. I know you are with me, but it hurts tremendously.

Your rod and your staff they comfort me.
I know this is not discipline. I know cancer did not grow here because of my sin. I know this, but I am still tempted to ask what I did to deserve this. Will you show me in real tangible ways how you are protecting me right now? Will you give me the comfort of seeing your protection? Will you show how you are guiding me through this physical, mental, emotional, and spiritual pain? If you will not show me your protection and guidance, will you give me faith that I do not have. Help me

believe you are doing this for my good. I want worldly comfort, but I know and believe your comfort is what I need.

You prepare a table before me in the presence of my enemies. You anoint my head with oil. My cup overflows.
This death at work in my body is my enemy. It has never been more clear who my enemy is. Remind me in this death that you are inviting me to feast right now on your goodness and mercy. Thank you for making me yours. I do not deserve this anointing. Thank you that you not only give me what I need, but you provide a cup overflowing with the joy of sitting at your table.

Only God's goodness and steadfast love shall pursue me all the days of my life.
I want to run away from all of this and from you as well. I do not want to face this pain. Thank you for chasing me down when my heart yearns to escape. Thank you for never giving up on me no matter how far and how often I wander. Thank you that when you chase me down, it is to restore me to your love.

And I shall dwell in the house of the LORD always and forever.
Does this future promise help me today? I know you have made your home in my heart and these promises are true right now, but I want an end to suffering. Jesus, how long do I have to wait? Give me hope today with the promise of forever without tears, pain, and suffering.

———

Now it's your turn.

The LORD is my shepherd; I have all I need.

He makes me lie down in green pastures. He leads me beside still waters. He restores my soul.

He leads me in paths of righteousness for his name's sake.

Even though I walk through the valley of the shadow of death I will fear no evil, for you are with me; your rod and your staff, they comfort me.

You prepare a table before me in the presence of my enemies; you anoint my head with oil; my cup overflows.

Only God's good and steadfast love shall pursue me all the days of my life, and I shall dwell in the house of the LORD always and forever.

Share what you wrote here with a trusted friend, family member, pastor, or counselor. You are not alone —Jesus the Good Shepherd is with you always. He also gives you others to walk with through this valley.

NOTES

Introduction

1. S. Lloyd-Jones, *The Jesus Storybook Bible*, (Michigan: Zondervan 2007), 331
2. *Your Lord knows best all those in the heavens and the earth. And We have surely favored some prophets above others, and to David He gave the Psalms.* —Quran 17:55

How Can We Suffer Well?

1. D. Kidner, *Psalms 1–72*, (Illinois: IVP 1973), 109
2. Brown, Driver, Briggs, *Hebrew and English Lexicon of the OT* (Massachusetts: Associated Publishers), 217–18
3. D. Kidner, *Psalms 1–72*, (Illinois: IVP 1973), 109\–110
4. C. F. Keil, F. Delitzsch, *Commentary on The OT Vol 5 Psalms*, (Hendrickson 2006), 207.
5. W. Keller, *A Shepherd looks at Psalm 23*, (Michigan: Zondervan 2007), 41–42
6. https://www.merriam-webster.com/dictionary/platitude
7. C. F. Keil, F. Delitzsch, *Commentary on The OT, Vol 5 Psalms*, (Massachusetts: Hendrickson 2006), 208.

How Can A Good God Allow Suffering?

1. https://books.google.com/ngrams/graph?
    content=comfort&year_
2. Pink Floyd. "Comfortably Numb." The Wall. Columbia, 1980. Digital
3. Tim Keller, *Counterfeit Gods*, (New York: Dutton 2009), 64

How Can We Suffer with Hope?

1. S. Lloyd-Jones, *The Jesus Storybook Bible* (Michigan: Zondervan 2007), 331

The Good Shepherd

1. Robert Robinson. "Come Thou Fount of Every Blessing." 1758. Public Domain

2. C. S. Lewis, *Letters to Malcolm, Chiefly on Prayer* (New York: Harper Collins 1992).

ACKNOWLEDGMENTS

I always read this section in a book. Perhaps because it humanizes the author and connects me to him or her through their connection with the people that were a part of their writing process. I particularly appreciate when the author has something witty or clever to say about their friends and family. Sorry to disappoint but my acknowledgements are sentimental because of how thankful I am for those who have given of themselves to make this happen.

Working with Storied Publishing and White Blackbird Books has given me more than publishing. They have given me friendship. Doug Serven's encouragement and care through this process has made even the difficult work of editing a fulfilling process.

Details are not my strength, and I am grateful for friends that have helped along the way making this more polished than it would have been had I done it alone. These friends have also given valuable feedback on arranging my thoughts and bringing clarity where there was confusion. Thank you Jessica Ribera, April Willets, and Bo Stapler for giving your time and encouragement.

I have dealt with chronic fatigue for much of my adult life and have not had the focus to sit and write at this length. Dr. Sarah Stewart has listened well and given me the help I have needed. This book would not have happened otherwise. Thank you Dr. Stewart.

Encouragement through this process has been crucial. Thank you Chris Talley, Dennis Hermerding, Greg Blosser, Jason Barrie, Rolf Meintjes, Brad Anderson, Travis Marsh, and Stephen Baldwin.

My children have kept me here. I am so honored they call me Dad. Abi, Nate, Naomi, and Mirriam, I love you more than I could ever express. But I will keep trying to express that love. Thank you for giving me a reason to write.

I had to learn to suffer with contentment. I learned to find joy in Christ when there was not anything happy. I did not expect any more beauty, hope, freedom and love. Then God brought Robin into my life. Thank you Robin for wanting more for me than you do for yourself. Thank you for loving and encouraging me so well. Thank you for making a life for us full of hope, joy, and grace.

ABOUT THE AUTHOR

Rob Wootton has served the Church for over twenty-five years as a pastor and campus minister in Montana, Virginia, Washington, and Missouri. He has a BFA in Art Education from Virginia Commonwealth University and an MDiv from Covenant Theological Seminary. He has been ordained in the Presbyterian Church in America since 2004. Rob is married to Robin, and they have four children. After family and ministry, Rob enjoys time outside in the mountains and the ocean. Snowboarding, surfing, rock climbing, sailing, and fly fishing are some of his favorite pursuits, but you will also find him playing, coaching, or watching soccer.

ABOUT WHITE BLACKBIRD BOOKS

White blackbirds are extremely rare, but they are real. They are blackbirds that have turned white over the years as their feathers have come in and out over and over again. They are a redemptive picture of something you would never expect to see but that has slowly come into existence over time.

There is plenty of hurt and brokenness in the world. There is the hopelessness that comes in the midst of lost jobs, lost health, lost homes, lost marriages, lost children, lost parents, lost dreams, loss.

But there also are many white blackbirds. There are healed marriages, children who come home, friends who are reconciled. There are hurts healed, children fostered and adopted, communities restored. Some would call these events entirely natural, but really they are unexpected miracles.

The books in this series are not commentaries, nor are they meant to be the final word. Rather, they are a collage of biblical truth applied to current times and places. The authors share their poverty and trust the Lord to use their words to strengthen and encourage his people. Consider these books as entries into the discussion.

May this series help you in your quest to know Christ as he is found in the Gospel through the Scriptures. May you look for and even expect the rare white blackbirds of God's redemption through Christ in your midst. May you be thankful when you look down and see your feathers have turned. May you also rejoice when you see that others have been unexpectedly transformed by Jesus.

ALSO BY WHITE BLACKBIRD BOOKS

A Year With the New Testament: A Verse By Verse Daily Devotional

All Are Welcome: Toward a Multi-Everything Church

The Almost Dancer

Birth of Joy: Philippians

Choosing a Church: A Biblical and Practical Guide

Christ in the Time of Corona: Stories of Faith, Hope, and Love

Co-Laborers, Co-Heirs: A Family Conversation

Doing God's Work

Driven By Desire: Insatiable Longings, Incredible Promises, Infinite God

EmbRACE: A Biblical Study on Justice and Race

Ever Light and Dark: Telling Secrets, Telling the Truth

Everything Is Meaningless? Ecclesiastes

Faithful Doubt: Habakkuk

Heal Us Emmanuel: A Call for Racial Reconciliation, Representation, and Unity in the Church

Hear Us, Emmanuel: Another Call for Racial Reconciliation, Representation, and Unity in the Church

The Organized Pastor: Systems to Care for People Well

Questions of the Heart: Leaning In, Listening For, and Loving Well Toward True Identity in Christ

Rooted: The Apostles' Creed

A Sometimes Stumbling Life

To You I Lift Up My Soul: Confessions and Prayers

Urban Hinterlands: Planting the Gospel in Uncool Places

Follow storied.pub for titles and releases.

Made in the USA
Coppell, TX
15 December 2021

68733410R00066